BEST WISHES

by

Cynthia Rylant

photographs by

Carlo Ontal

 Richard C. Owen Publishers, Inc.
Katonah, New York

Richard C. Owen Publishers, Inc.
135 Katonah Avenue
Katonah, New York 10536

Library of Congress Cataloging-in-Publication Data

Rylant, Cynthia.
    Best wishes / by Cynthia Rylant ; photographs by Carlo Ontal.
        p.   cm. —(Meet the author)
    Summary: Children's author Cynthia Rylant describes her life and
writing process and how they are interwoven.
    ISBN 1-878450-20-4
    1. Rylant, Cynthia—Biography—Juvenile literature.   2. Authors,
American—20th century—Biography—Juvenile literature.
3. Children's literature—Authorship—Juvenile literature.
[1. Rylant, Cynthia.   2. Authors, American.]   I. Ontal, Carlo, ill.
II. Title.   III. Series: Meet the author (Katonah, N.Y.)
PS3568.Y55Z463   1992   NEDKSO11
813'.54—dc20
[B]   92-7796

The text type was set in Caslon 540.
Production supervision by Janice Boland
Book design by Kenneth J. Hawkey

Printed in the United States of America

9 8 7 6 5 4 3 2 1

Sometimes your best wishes really do come true.
When I was a little girl
I used to wish for a pretty house
with a big picture window,
a faithful dog who loved me,
cats,
and a chance to do something important.

I lived in West Virginia with my mother,
my two grandparents, my many aunts and uncles,
and my many more cousins.
Because we hadn't much money
(being a coal-mining family)
I did a lot of wishing for a lot of things.
And when I was grown, I got many of those things.
I got the house with the window,
the faithful dog, the cats.

And I also did something important:
I became a writer.
I read mostly comic books when I was growing up.
There was no library, no bookstore where I lived.
So I read comic books.
No one ever expected that to turn me into a writer.
But it helped. It made me love stories.

I roamed around a lot when I was growing up,
along the country dirt roads at first,
where friends like Miss Maggie Ziegler
lived in her old log house.
Then later I roamed a little town named Beaver,
with its market, its filling station,
its hardware store.

No one expected my roaming
to turn me into a writer, either.
But it helped.
I saw what was happening inside houses.
I heard what people were saying outside stores.

I met a lot of animals.
And all these things
I remembered when I became a writer,
and I put them into books.

Today I live in a small house
in a small town in Ohio.
The town's name is Kent.
I like it because
here I can walk down a little street
and say hello to store owners
just like I used to as a child.

I have a great son named Nate
(he's really "Nathaniel,"
after a famous writer).
He keeps our house alive
with his music, his video games,
his film-making, and his tussles with the dogs.

That's another wish that came true:
the faithful dog.
Her name is Martha Jane
and she loves me.
I even have a little dog who loves me, too:
Her name is Leia.
Martha Jane loves stuffed animals,
tennis balls, and my bed.

Leia loves kitties, and lucky for her we have two:
Edward Velvetpaws and Blueberry,
and they mostly love eating.
Edward is an outside cat so he wears a little bell.
At night I call for him out the door
and I hear *Tinkle Tinkle Tinkle Tinkle*
and I know he's on his way home.

My days are mostly quiet days.
I help Nate fold his papers
for his paper route at 5:30 a.m.
When he goes off to school, I have a cup of tea
and I read or I answer mail from children.

Then the dogs and I go for our walk
in Towner's Woods.
Martha runs ahead, Leia pokes behind,
and I'm always somewhere in the middle.
This is my best time of day.

If it is a day when I feel like writing,
I will come home and sit quietly outside
with a pen and some paper.
I daydream.
Then I write.

Usually what I write surprises me.
The idea comes fast
and the words are often quite clear in my head.
Before I get up again,
I've written a new picture book.
And I always know whether it's good or not.
I just know.

But I don't write every day.
I save up my thoughts
for weeks at a time, even months.

When it's time to write again, I'll know,
and maybe the story will be a made up story
(like *All I See*).
Or maybe it will be a story
that comes from my real life.
The Henry and Mudge characters
come from my own son Nate
and a big dog named Mudge I used to know.

I like doing other things, too.

I plant flowers.

I fill the bird feeders.

I might work on a quilt,
or I might go to the movies.
(I *love* the movies.)
I have two or three close friends
and I might visit with one of them.
I even like tidying up my house.
I'm always changing something in my house.
My friends think it's funny.
Every time they come over, something's different.
I tell them I'm releasing creative energy
when I move the furniture around.
Really I'm just having fun.

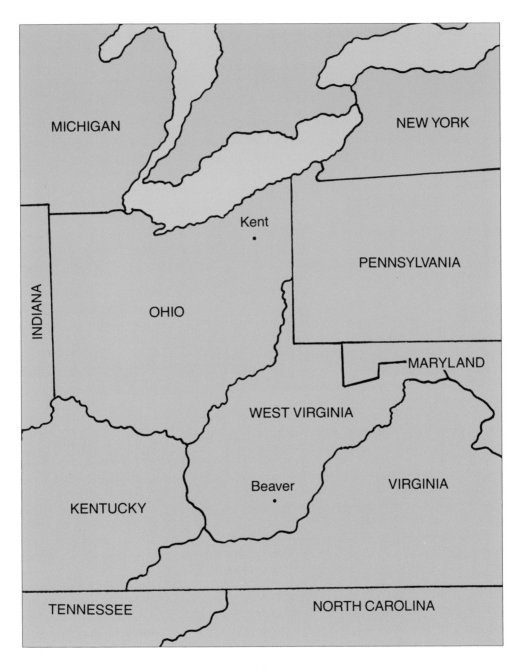

MICHIGAN

NEW YORK

Kent

PENNSYLVANIA

INDIANA

OHIO

MARYLAND

WEST VIRGINIA

Beaver

VIRGINIA

KENTUCKY

TENNESSEE

NORTH CAROLINA

A few times during the year
I go back to West Virginia to see my family.
My grandmother still lives
in the same little house I wrote about
in *When I Was Young in the Mountains*.

Those relatives in *The Relatives Came*
still drive up to visit.
Uncle Dean still plants this year's garden.
And when I sleep
in my mother's trailer among the trees,
I hear the sounds of night in the country.

One of the best parts of my visit
is sitting with Grandmama
at her kitchen table and talking.
I like to find out who's been doing what
since my last visit.

And I can't wait for supper
and some of my mom's good country cornbread.

I try to do a little work for them while I'm there.
I like to take Grandmama to the grocery
or plant flowers in her yard.

And, of course, I always bring
plenty of copies of my newest book.
They're all very proud of my books.

When it's time to leave, everybody hugs me
and tells me to drive careful
and come back real soon.
They wave as I drive off down the road
and we all feel a little sad for a while.

But when I get back to my own house,
Martha Jane is wiggling with joy,
Leia is running in circles,
light is pouring through the picture window
as the cats open their sleepy eyes,
and the best of all wishes comes true.
I'm home.

Other Books by Cynthia Rylant

All I See; *An Angel for Solomon Singer*; *Appalachia: The Voices of Sleeping Birds*; *Birthday Presents*; *A Blue-Eyed Daisy* (YA); *But I'll Be Back Again: An Album*; *Children of Christmas*; *Every Living Thing*; *A Fine White Dust* (YA); *the Henry and Mudge* books; *A Kindness* (YA); *Miss Maggie*; *Missing May* (YA); *Mr. Grigg's Work*; *Night in the Country*; *The Relatives Came*; *Soda Jerk*; *This Year's Garden*; *Waiting to Waltz: A Childhood*; *When I Was Young in the Mountains*.

About the Photographer

Carlo Ontal is a freelance photographer who likes to play with light. He lives in New York City. Carlo has worked with Cynthia Rylant before, and enjoyed doing this book so much that he hopes to do more children's books in the future.

Acknowledgments

Illustration on page 8 from *Miss Maggie* by Cynthia Rylant, illustrated by Thomas DiGrazia. Copyright © 1983 by Thomas DiGrazia for illustrations. Used by permission of Dutton Children's Books, a division of Penguin Books USA Inc. Illustration on page 19 from *All I See* by Cynthia Rylant, illustrated by Peter Catalonotto. Copyright © 1988 by Peter Catalonotto for illustrations. Used by permission of Orchard Books, New York.

Meet the Author titles

Rafe Martin   *A Storyteller's Story*
Cynthia Rylant   *Best Wishes*
Jane Yolen   *A Letter from Phoenix Farm*